BEING DEAF AT THE TOWER OF BABEL

BEING DEAF AT THE TOWER OF BABEL

by Thomas Ronald Vaughan

Poems

RESOURCE *Publications* · Eugene, Oregon

BEING DEAF AT THE TOWER OF BABEL
Poems

Wipf & Stock
An Imprint of Wipf and Stock Publishers
199 W. 8th Ave., Suite 3
Eugene, OR 97401

www.wipfandstock.com

PAPERBACK ISBN: 978-1-5326-9159-1
HARDCOVER ISBN: 978-1-5326-9160-7
EBOOK ISBN: 978-1-5326-9161-4

Manufactured in the U.S.A.

Especially for Jayne
who gave me
poems
without knowing it.

I Have Adored You

I have adored you mouth to mouth.
I have adored you mouth to ear.
I have adored you hand to breast.
I have adored you tear to tear.

I have adored you miles apart
In lonely rooms, for days and days,
And when I could not see your face
I have adored your lively ways.

Beside you on this couch of ease
And safety, in our slow decline,
Toward no possessing, no regret:
I have adored what is not mine.

The Creation of Adam

And lying by the rivers deep
There yet unformed did Adam sleep.
While little fishes played in schools
The Creator made molecules.

He made two hands, she made a heart.
He fit together every part.
She made two lungs, a chest that heaved.
Into the lungs the Lord God breathed.

The creature standing by the river
Coughed and gasped, began to shiver.
The eyelids rose, he fixed his eyes
And gazed out on his "Paradise."

What wild thoughts must have filled that brain
As it beheld the strange terrain:
The first two eyes, the first to see
The handwork of eternity!

But long he stood there unaffected,
Knowing nothing, not directed:
Silent and dumb, he racked his mind,
That first colossal Frankenstein.

Meanwhile, the watching Lord of Hosts
Said, "Now!", and then the Holy Ghost
Descended near and touched the man
And whispered low, "Child: Understand!"

Emily Dickinson

So mystically pallid,
Coquettishly demure,
So bittersweet in waiting,
But that was not the cure.

While casting out for meaning
For where to start and end,
She wrote her plaintive anthem
And gave it to the wind.

Emily Dickinson, poet, 1830-1886

Things Without Names

I

There was "a love that dare not speak its name,"
As Oscar Wilde rode off to Reading Gaol,
And Alfred Douglas flitted here and there
To offer everything he had for sale.

II

Do things exist which do not have a word
To make them so or not, or give them sound?
Who named it when an ancient, angry man
Sat up and spilled his seed upon the ground?

III

As docile creatures passed his way to learn
Their names, which would eternally abide,
The drowsy Adam paused and strained to hear
A strange vocabulary in his side.

Friends Oscar Wilde, 1854-1900,
and Lord Alfred Douglas, 1870-1945

Lola

Lola on the bed reclining,
Marketer to boy and man.
Thinking of financial planning,
Burning cigarette in hand.

Smiling as they smooth and straighten,
Tucking evidence away,
Winking as they turn to leave her,
Vanishing into the day.

Lola folds in silk and satin,
Confidante of man and boy.
Queen royale of all that pulses,
Matriarch of every toy.

Being Deaf at The Tower of Babel

I

I came because they told me with a sign
That some great god had let his voice be heard.
I came because though deaf I am not blind.
There are more ways than one to hear the word.

I walk with those who speak of where we go
With such anticipation in their eyes
That though I cannot hear the words I know
That soon some mighty monument will rise

Before us in the desert like the sun!
And if I understand it right they say
The work has only recently begun,
And we will not be home for many a day.

I know their testimony will prove true!
This god is calling us to some great task.
I'm old but I will do what I can do,
And that is all that any god can ask.

There will be water needed for the brick.
And though I'm bent my shoulders still are strong.
There doubtless will be many who fall sick;
They will be glad an old man came along.

II

But who are these returning on the way
In opposite direction from the spot
To which we go? What do they try to say?
My friends should understand them but do not!

"Turn back! Turn back!" Are these the words they show?
"Go home! Go back!" Do these weak eyes deceive?
Where do these incoherent strangers go?
This lack of faith I struggle to believe.

Dear ones proceed, for see how far we've come!
Six days and nights we've fought against these sands.
But who will follow one who's deaf and dumb,
And has only the words of two old hands.

Not one remains with me. I am alone.
They melt into the distance like this day.
But I will go. I must, I must go on.
The holy site cannot be far away.

And so, on toward the dying desert light
An old man stumbled and an old man wept.
And somewhere in the silence of the night
He made a sign to heaven, and he slept.

After Eden

How dare you dare to tempt me—
Unmitigated gall!
Your world began to tremble
And mine began to fall.

The serpent wiles were cunning,
Allurement with a smile.
And when he left he left her
The meaning of beguile.

I sweat and scratch and labor,
And curse the leaden sky,
And when the womb is opened,
I pound the fist and cry.

Pyromania

Beyond a mother's loose attire
He traced his movement into fire.
He closed his eyes and there he saw
The insight couple with desire.

Whose woods they were he thought he knew.
It did not matter as he threw
The lighted package in the straw.
It glowed. He smiled. His body grew.

A Death in the Neighborhood

There is the house. There is the man.
His days have fast flown by.
He has his youth, but not his health.
It is his time to die.

It is his time for death, they say,
And surely he must leave.
But as a man of no renown
There will be few to grieve.

Then I will grieve untimely death;
Yes, I will keep the day.
We did not know the other's name,
Just nodded on the way.

And I will search expanding skies
Where those of no renown
Are everlastingly ensconced
In stars that don't fall down.

Noah in Old Age

"Never again! A boat of any kind!
That constant rocking on a muddy sea,
The things that float by in your wildest dreams
Sometimes I thought would get the best of me.

Odd animals stuck in their stinking pens,
The acrid smoke that made my senses halt—
You call it an adventure if you will!"
So Noah drank and drank. His life was salt.

The Glance

Across the crowded room
A desperation glance.
They sail for home today.
This is the final chance.

A woman you have loved,
And she in love with you.
Two marriages in stone—
The glance will have to do.

Before I Learned

Before I learned the politics of war,
To ask who are we fighting and what for,
I would have charged to kill them in the trench;
I would have crawled to kill them inch by inch.

Before I learned its rich economy,
I thought of carnage quite indifferently.
I would have prized a napalm-dotted sky,
And cheered as on a hot Fourth of July.

Before I slammed into the man of peace,
Who said that wars inside and out must cease,
I would have swaggered forward with a spear
And turned it just to see the sweet flesh tear.

Jericho

In Jericho a sadness falls,
The fortress power is gone.
Where is the prophet-soldier who
Rebuilds to make it strong?

He has gone west with Israel,
And Ai is in sight.
The weeping heard in Jericho
Will echo there tonight.

Who orders this destructive path,
By what right do they come
To claim the land of Palestine
For an eternal home?

It was a revelation voice,
A frightful promise made,
And every word was thus believed,
And every word obeyed.

The women wail in Jericho.
They rock their dusty dead.
But Israel wipes clean its sword,
And does not turn its head.

Jonquils

I placed my coin on jonquils
For I could pay the cost.
Since jonquils bloom each springtime,
No money would be lost.

But March gave way to April
And April turned to May.
My friend demanded payment;
Disturbed, I had to pay.

I gazed out on the meadow,
So barren, brown, and dead
And thought of blowing jonquils
And all I'd rashly said.

A thing one takes for granted
Must not be taken so.
Will jonquils bloom in springtime?
Well, maybe yes, or no.

Elijah

Elijah sat in Horeb's cave
And huddled in his fear,
But then an apparition came
And asked, "Why are you here?"

Elijah said, "I am, alone,
Of all the people, true.
But Jezebel will have my life,
As she the prophets slew."

But It said, "Look!" and then, behold,
A mighty wind blew by,
And then an earthquake with its roar
Broke rocks and shook the sky.

And then, again, the clouds on fire!
Elijah looked to see.
But God was not in either of
The spectacles of three.

And as the prophet pondered on
Strange sights without a choice
Of seeing God go by, he stopped,
And, lo! a still, small voice.

Absence Makes the Heart

I'm told that hearts grow fonder
When hearts are far apart,
Then hearts at home and hearts at war
Should beat as if one heart.

But I am much the wiser
Than to believe it so,
For I recall a friend of mine
Who lost his heart, I know.

The war was worth the fighting,
Or that is what he thought.
Two hearts embraced and kissed good-bye,
And he sailed as he ought.

For duty and for honor
He struggled and he bled,
And more than once upon the field
Was given up for dead.

But far from where he struggled,
And far from where he strove,
Another war was raging on
In hearts confused by love.

So when he travelled homeward
To put his wounds away,
She looked at him and he at her
And all was changed that day.

I'm reassured that absence
Is good for healthy hearts.
Such wisdom must be lost on one
That beats in fits and starts.

The Charge

He held him in his arms
As life drifted away,
With nothing much to do
And even less to say.

The charge was poorly planned,
And men began to fall.
Retreat was sounded soon,
It made no sense at all.

But that is what you do
When nations arm to fight.
You charge and then retreat
Without a wrong or right.

And so he held him close,
And held him till he died,
Who never met before,
Eternally allied.

Slaughter of the Children

The pacifists of Bethlehem
Bowed as the soldiers came
To snatch the children one by one
And play their slashing game.

The mothers screamed as babies fell
Before them in their blood.
But pacifists sat down to pray,
And prayed the words they could.

Saint Joseph in the distance turned
To hear sad Rachel weep,
Then shooed the holy family on
Toward Egypt and toward sleep.

But as he walked on Gaza's Road
Beside his wife and son,
He wondered, had no dream occurred,
What would he then have done.

And back in cowed Jerusalem
The arguments increase
That he would be a man of war,
Or, no, a prince of peace.

After the Temple

You listen to me even if you are
A Son of God born under some bright star—
Until you do whatever you will do,
You live with us, and we take care of you.

Now, give an explanation if you can—
Why did you not go with us, but you ran!
And though we called and called for you to stay,
You followed your obsession, come what may!

What do you think that we were doing when
You spent three days conversing with your friends?
I don't care where it was, or what you said.
My goodness, child, we feared you might be dead.

OK! All right! We can and will forget.
But do not end this conversation yet.
Just reassure me on this very day—
You will be subject till you go away!

Though Those Who Go for Witnesses

Though those who go for witnesses
Must swear upon the Word,
My lips are sealed, I will not talk,
I won't say what I heard.

I'll raise my hand, so help me God,
But that is all I'll do.
For I will never once repeat
The words I heard from you.

And if they quiz me years from now,
Again I will declaim:
"Who pushed the dagger through your heart!"
I will not know your name.

Cana of Galilee

They think that I have come here to affirm
Two children who profess "eternal love,"
To comment on this earthy institution
Declared as an ordainment from above.

Well, I was there and I do not remember
A thing about parental prearrangement,
That they, beyond all others, know what's best,
And offspring merely passively assent.

But nonetheless the wine is very good—
A vintage red, with wonderful hors d'oeuvres.
And what a table spread with fine delights,
Which each slave smiles and dutifully serves.

My guess is they will say that I was here,
And just because I was the thing is blessed.
I should have simply waved as I passed by,
And let them fume and argue as they guessed.

No, I would not have come had she not said,
In her perfected, irritating way,
That these dear neighbors would not understand
If we had other plans on this quaint day.

Now here she comes, a frowning, dismal face.
I stare into the ground and then look up:
"And are you having fun, my Mother, dear?
Why thrust at me that unclean, empty cup?"

To Alan Seegar
(d. 1916, WWI)

You kept your rendezvous with death
When spring came north that deadly year.
I am assured that your last breath
Conceded not a line to fear.

I've often thought of what you knew,
The horrors your prim words belied.
You must have kept that rendezvous
A hundred times before you died.

Poet, Alan Seegar, 1888-1916

The Farmyard

There is a farmyard in my mind
Where through the lens of age,
The children that I used to know
Play on its friendly stage.

I shout for them to clap and sing.
I tell them, "Smile, be glad!"
But I remember playing there,
And playing there was sad.

We cannot blame the place or land.
We cannot blame the day.
The players and their lines came from
Dark houses, far away.

The Mystic

Swinging through my forests of desire,
Effortlessly touching limb by limb,
Every branch and twig bursts into fire,
Canopies irrupt in praise of Him!

Diving in my deeper reefs of passion,
Awed by vasts of lusty life to see.
Swimming in the colors of amazement,
Grace-encapsulated gifts, and free!

Straining on my mountains of atonement,
Valleys shout in perfect harmony!
Constellations bow in strict oblation
Spiraling into this ecstasy!

Salome

Salome was proficient in a style
That caused a petty potentate to squirm.
His eyes were transfixed on her shapely form
And things he thought once dead might become firm.

Arousal by a woman or by wine
Can generate extravagant decrees.
And even if your wife is sitting near
The drunken slurring speaks to what it sees.

"I give you anything your heart desires,
For you delight me and it is no matter."
"Thank you most graciously, my sweet, sweet king—
The head of John, called Baptist, on a platter!"

"See to it guards, and see to it right swiftly.
Now, come Salome, come and take my hand."
"Please let me dance until the deed is over,
And we are no more troubled by this man."

It was a night of music and of kings
With food and wine to lavish on their peers.
But ribaldry can yield the strangest thoughts
To question what one sees and what one hears:

For did she not caress the golden plate,
And did she with her sensuous fingertips,
Drag blood across the rim and hold it light,
To suck between her fulsome, painted lips?

The sober morning found him more perplexed.
He could not quite recall what happened next,
For did he retch to see that now instead
Of his she kissed the dripping, severed head?

Nicodemus

"The Holy Spirit blows
Among us like the wind."
And Nicodemus strained
To comprehend his friend.

But as he slinked along
And thought of what was said,
No stone was rolled way,
So he went off to bed.

Back in the light he sensed
Some power fix their course,
And later he became
The qualified resource.

As painful months groaned on,
Sad Joseph called to say,
"You bring the spice and myrrh.
We wrap the dead today."

And as those mourners tucked
The body in the shroud,
O, how the wind began,
And, o, the wind was loud.

When Christ Shot Herod

When Christ shot Herod full of holes
The people gasped, and said,
"You'd better watch your mouth, young man,
Or soon you will be dead."

But he just smiled and fired on,
For he was making plans,
And orchestrating everything,
Conjoining God's demands.

Now Herod was a crafty fox,
And copied every word,
And then reviewed the manuscript
But changed what had been heard

To fit his pre-conditioned goal
Of power—tight, secure.
No insurrecting carpenter
Could challenge and endure.

So plan met plan and who can say
Which one was best conceived,
When Pilate washed his hands to hear,
"Kill him! We don't believe!"

Military Funeral

A gathering of flowers
And friends are told goodbye.
She speaks the "dust and ashes,"
And mourners stare and sigh.

To words both old and poignant,
They listen and they know
That many heard before them
And lie here, row on row.

She prays with Father Newman,
"O Lord support us all,
And grant a peaceful lodging
In your safe mansion hall."

Old soldiers fire old rifles.
A flag cantoned to stay,
Is handed to the family
To read day after day.

We spread the gathered flowers
Upon the sacred loam.
We go into our churches,
They go into their home.

Across the field of sorrow
A weary sun resigns,
But it will come tomorrow
And she repeat her lines.

John Henry Newman, 1801-1890,
Roman Catholic Cardinal

The Prodigal

My God, I dread this coming fateful scene!
How can I meet my Father face to face?
How I am longing for what might have been—
My coming home in honor and in grace,
In joy for one who glorified his name—
But I am coming home in rags and shame.

There is the house, and there the man I fear.
We cannot suffer this, and I must go.
But now he greets the stranger coming near—
The son who slept with hogs! He must not know.
I hear a faithful brother's mocking laugh,
But do I also hear, "A robe! A calf!"

The Sea
(after John Masefield)

When tides come in by morning,
And ships set out to sea,
I stand and watch them sailing.
That is no place for me.

I stay on terra firma.
I know how it behaves.
I am no brash apostle;
I do not walk on waves.

The call to other duties
I hear, and must obey.
I scan the blue horizon.
I turn, and am away.

But days and nights from this one,
Shut in my refuge home,
The sea will whisper, "Seaward,"
And it knows I will come.

John Masefield, poet, 1878-1967,
wrote *Sea Fever*

Upper Room

"Where shall I sit?" he wondered.
"Where shall I sit?" asked he.
"Come here and sit you softly,
And lean your head on me."

And so began an evening
For one about to lie,
And one about to treasure,
And one about to die.

Hopkins' "Blue-Bleak Embers"

How I have been enchanted by that phrase
For nameless ranks old fires of earth did raze,
Or wars, or pillages, or deadly plague—
They marched, inevitably, to the grave.
In nameless fields, forgotten still, they lie.
Their illegible tombstones face the sky.

The sweetness of their plight, best told by Gray,
Echoed across the heartstrings to his day.
To Hopkins' heart they died but were not dead,
Like embers, dark, whose cores were quiver-red.
Their souls were not extinguished in the sod:
They burst into the glory of their God.

Gerard Manley Hopkins, poet, 1844-1889;
Thomas Gray, poet, 1716-1771

Beyond These Fields

Beyond these fields dark clouds arise,
And soon there will be rain.
Sharp lightning flashes angrily,
Rough wind disturbs the grain.

I see in waves approaching me
Our destined meeting sure.
There is not shelter anywhere—
I stand and must endure.

I stand and must endure alone,
And never own the thought
That others will endure for me,
Or may, or could, or ought.

I stand where roads have taken me;
At every turn, I chose.
And if I face uncaring skies,
My choices gave me those.

"Into each life some rain must fall,"
A trite consensus yields.
But true is true, for I have gone
Abroad in weathered fields.

Suicide

The night he kicked the stool away
And swung so gently there,
His wife was in the living room,
His daughter on the stair.

He'd thought of all that made him laugh
And what had made him cry.
But all in all was not enough,
And so this brusque good-bye.

Thick, sturdy rafters held secure
Till she came down to see
This closing chapter of a life—
A clouded mystery.

He left no note or word to tell
Why this dark deed was done.
(Good neighbors said they thought they knew—
The war he could have won.)

She asked herself ten thousand times
But no sure answer came.
As did the grieving family—
They answered all the same.

So, still the ancient plague lives on
And God alone knows why
Some end the sad soliloquy:
"Now, one of us must die!"

The Ascent

A mountain looms before me,
And I must scale its height.
And if I start off early
I may be home by night.

I may be home by evening,
And if I can, I will.
This mountain is forbidding,
But I must try it still.

For on the far and rough side
Abides the thing I need,
The prize that gives life meaning,
In which I most believe.

How it got to the dark side,
Abandoning me here,
Is not now worth the telling,
But is to me quite clear.

It happened, and I left it,
But now I hear the call
To go back and retrieve it,
Or what is lost is—all.

This must be my best effort,
From everything I know.
Here is the mountain looming.
I look up and I go.

The Garden

The agony of hunger,
The wretchedness of thirst!
But friends who will betray you,
I think that is the worst.

I think it is most painful
To trust and then to learn
For thirty coins of silver
Their hearts and faces turn.

And in the night-dressed garden
Where tear-stained rocks are found,
A voice is heard, "Hail, Master!"
And kisses curse the ground.

A friend who will betray you,
Himself betrayed by fate,
Has not a friend to turn to,
Repents, but cannot wait.

The agony of hunger,
The wretchedness of thirst,
But those who will not trust you,
I think that is the worst.

As We Have From Our Youth

As we have from our youth,
And now we both are old,
Lay down, my dearest dear,
The night is dark and cold.

Do you remember when
The world was young and warm,
And we acted as if
That world could bring no harm?

O, we have lived since then,
And life has taught us more
Than ever we had dreamed
Two lives had had in store.

So come, my dearest dear,
And let us rest and sleep.
The night is dark and cold,
And we have hearts to keep.

Carravagio

In his great work, "The Taking of the Christ",
The arm of Judas is not long enough
To catch the man, much less to reel him in:
A necessary trait for fishermen.

And thus appears the boisterous gendarme,
With his obnoxious bellicosity,
Deluded that his crass, profane commands
Could phase the figure staring at his hands.

The scene is much too crowded for the scene.
Rough men are pressing in; the air is stale.
Poor Peter, certifiably insane,
Runs to the darkness and begins to wail.

Carravagio, Italian Artist, 1571-1610

Cupid

Show me where the arrow hit you!
Did it leave a wound to scar?
He is quite an able marksman,
Decimating near and far.

But I see no blood or breakage,
Nothing torn or ripped apart.
Yet, you will be gone by morning;
Sad, the kill shot struck the heart.

Grief

There is a grief that does not end,
It snaps the heart in two.
But multitudes have worn its wound,
So grief is nothing new.

If hearts could choose, then hearts would choose,
And grief would not abide,
And hearts would make their way about
With joy and peace beside.

But grief is never far away
When lively hearts begin
To think that they are safe and sound
And it cannot come in.

As Simon from the countryside
Stopped on the road to see
Three men condemned drag by, he said,
"And what is that to me?"

But sometimes Roman soldiers are
The purveyors of loss,
And sometimes Roman soldiers shout,
"You! Come and take the cross!"

Yes, life has unexpected things
When men are passing by,
And some are coming from their fields,
And some go out to die.

There is a grief that does not end,
It creeps into the soul.
And there erects a domicile
Where men and it grow old.

Domestic Violence I

The mother begged for mercy.
The father offered none.
He was the savior holding
The resurrection gun.

Why drunk men talk of spirit,
I swear, I do not know.
She wears a cemetery,
He paces on Death Row.

Centurion

I had no way of knowing,
If ever know I can,
That after such commotion,
He was an honest man.

He did not curse or grumble.
He did not roll his eyes.
He said to one beside him,
"Today, in Paradise."

So if right now they amble
Upon some other shore,
I have no way of knowing.
I think of it no more.

Judas

The gates of Hell swing outward,
The gates of Hell swing in.
He thought he heard them calling,
"Disgorge yourself of sin!"

Below, he saw a valley,
And in it was a hill,
And on it were three crosses,
And they were killing still.

But he was on the high ground,
And Hell was very near,
And he was there already.
He turned and did not fear.

Yes, gates of Hell swing inward,
And gates of Hell swing out,
And they compete with crosses
For souls sick and distraught.

Vietnam Redux

I shot the women first, he said,
I killed the women first.
In all the villages we took
The women were the worst.

But then the conversation turned
From strategy to pain,
And sobbing into trembling hands
In crushing self-disdain.

It was my time for wordlessness,
I who could ramble on
Of dogmas, creeds, things to believe
To build a world upon.

But here a world was crashing down,
Its sure foundations swayed.
And in the rubble one lost man,
A Samson shorn and shaved.

Some Saviors see and come and save;
Some Saviors stand and stare
In deedless, worthless empathy:
Such Christs are everywhere.

The Snow Road

Had it not snowed, I had not seen
The road along the riverbank.
I am not often in these parts,
And I had thought it merely sank
Beyond the oaks, and did not cross
The water, which is deep and wide,
But curved back in the distance to
The place where I am standing. I'd
Imagined nothing of the sort—
That here there was an ancient ford
Where ancient travelers found the port
Of call for one small craft, aboard
Which all of their possessions moved
Till safely on the other side,
Continued westward to the land
Where westward dreams had lived or died.

I am not able now to tell
Why, as I walked this wintry day,
I came to where I once had thought
The road had gently turned away
And disappeared without a trace.
I know that is not what roads do,
But toil and care of life can keep
The mind from seeing what is true.
So, even if in summertime
I have to cross the water here,
And if I must and if I reach
That shore, and I am standing there,
I think that in my heart of hearts
I will not wonder where I go.
No, I will take the sunken road
Marked clearly by the light of snow.

Easter

On resurrection morning
A tension fills the heart—
Shall we prepare for leaving?
What stays when we depart?

It is the old, old wisdom,
The self we cannot save.
And granite asks the question,
"A garden or a grave?"

She quizzed a man she noticed,
"Where have you laid him, Sir?"
She grappled with confusion.
He did not answer her,

Then spoke: she could not hold him,
But he must roam about.
He gave her words to tell them.
She left him with a shout.

On resurrection morning
A tension fills the soul,
And we attend in silence
To stories we are told.

Her Hair Was Dark

Her hair was dark, her eyes were blue,
They twinkled like the stars.
He told her all that he would do
When he came from the wars.

She held her breath and said her prayers
And waited day by day.
The guns grew silent, truce was signed,
But yet he stayed away.

He stayed away and truth be told,
He lived another life,
Not far from where she thought that she
Agreed to be his wife.

She did her chores, she trifled, and
She watched the dusty lane
Where handsome soldiers wave goodbye,
But do not come again.

The hair grew white, the gait grew slow,
The dancing eyes grew dim.
But not to where she could not see
The visages of him.

All plans arranged, the dark eyes shut,
When he was brought to say
That he had known a younger girl
Some lives and miles away,

That he had planned to come and ask
If things had been all right,
But blinded soldiers without legs
Are not a welcome sight.

The tale is sad, the tale is true,
The once so strong and tall,
Told me through tears the wars he fought
Had changed nothing at all.

Domestic Violence II

If he had raised his hand,
She would have run away.
But he had only smiled,
So she agreed to stay.

And thus it all begins
And escalates until
She wonders what she did
To make the lover kill.

On Courting Mary After Easter

Your husband was a carpenter, I hear.
The son was quite impressive in his day.
Jerusalem still speaks of him, I fear.
Was he a Jew, or did he go astray?

No matter. I am here for earthly things.
My wife was taken from me, as you know.
A fever which the summer season brings
Unmercifully doomed her months ago.

I speak too much! I should not carry on,
Except to say that we have both known pain.
You have no one besides your youngest, John.
I crave the joys of hearth and home again.

I leave you to consider what I say.
Please send me word as soon as you are able.
Think on it as you eat this raw, first day.
I see the bread and wine upon your table.

Post-Traumatic Stress Disorder

I

Soldier, kneel, embrace your children —
Safe at home from shell and shot —
Then your anxious spouse in waiting
With the love that war forgot.

Cross the threshold, they will greet you,
Threshold crossed a thousand times.
Do not flinch at unsure touching —
They are trying to be kind.

II

Then, good soldier, tell your story —
Brace, you, for the shock they'll show.
You have reigned on fields of glory;
It is right for them to know!

Speak of flesh and parts of body —
Friend or foe, you could not tell.
You were brave and did your duty
In the very jaws of hell.

Line by line they rushed in fury;
Bending, but you did not break.
Tell them how they fell before you,
Fell, the lives you had to take.

III

Will it do you good to say it?
No, best not. It is too raw.
Now is not the time — or ever.
Just for you the things you saw.

So, goodnight, the party over,
Show them out, engage the latch.
Think of how they had to leave you:
"Death so near, but not a scratch!"

Now, as you lie down for resting
By the one you loved for long,
When dark scenes assail unbidden,
You are ready. You are strong.

St. Anthony

From stones he made a seat,
And on the seat he sat,
And peered into the dark,
And thought of this and that.

The wonder of it all
Is that he looked again,
For when he looked he saw
Vile demons urging sin.

Saint Anthony recoiled
And fell upon the ground
And panted as he rolled,
With an unearthly sound.

He scratched and kicked and clawed
And wrestled with a foe
Which touched him on the thigh
And would not let him go.

But when the hot sun rose,
The demons fled away,
And Anthony engaged
The liturgical day.

Yet as the hours droned on,
And dark shadows returned,
Saint Anthony prayed hard,
For, o, his body burned.

And on and on it went,
And every night they came,
And every night he fought,
And every night the same.

And so the mindless flesh
Beseiged the mindful soul,
And Anthony could not
Make of the two a whole.

Anthony of Egypt, 251-356,
a founder of monasticism

Monasteries

They built their monasteries in the world
To softly chant what is and what is not.
A backward glance and then a life was gone —
That world forgetting, by that world forgot.

Godiva

Austere in her adornment
She straddled horse and mane.
With Leofric's approval
She played a teasing game.

I am not sure or certain
If taxes fell or rose,
But Tom began his peeping,
Or, so the story goes.

Old Coventry will never
Forget the way she served,
Unseen but still imagined,
How civically she swerved.

Godiva and Leofric, of 11th century
Anglo-Saxon England

Gifts For You

Here is a dark but once familiar key.
I kept it for this reason, I suppose,
To open now the rough spare wooden chest,
And show these items not unknown to me.

This is a highly shopworn book on trees.
So often I have seen you stand and gaze;
Some pages cracked, the pictures still are clear.
I thought that you would like to look at these.

And this — a coin from some lost ancient land,
Which has the likeness of a scolding king.
His name is gone, but I can wish that then
It freely passed from hand to friendly hand.

And here a red and badly fraying bow.
It was atop a gift I gave you once,
That I have tried — but have forgotten now.
It simply was a time too long ago.

And look: a crumbling flower we pressed one day
From a green field I now recall we watched
Until the sun slid sleepily to earth,
And we took home, for what I cannot say.

I show you, too, this feather, glistening brown,
Which may have helped the bird we had then seen
Soaring above in vast and dizzy heights.
It landed at my feet when it fell down.

And you, no doubt, can place this fading card,
Wishing us all the best of everything,
That anniversary an age now past
When we so often said the year was hard.

The last, a simple sparkling granite stone
That lay for long beside the one small rise,
A tiny tombstone watching faithfully
The son we thought was ours and ours alone.

Regrettably, I have no more to share,
So I have gently placed these here for you,
And someday you can hold them one by one
To do whatever then seems right and fair.

I do not know why I so long have kept
This foolish trove among more useful things,
But I have found that when I've stopped to look,
I have sat in a lonely chair and wept.

Chiusdino, Italy

The noble knight Galgano,
While searching for his Lord,
Soon found he had no crucifix
And so he used a sword.

A sword in rock embedded
Can serve a hermit well.
A crucifix in any form
May save a soul from Hell.

It still is found encrusted
Beneath the vaulted dome
Where saintly knight Galgano
Sat down and made a home.

The visitors are dazzled
For there it is to see—
The sharp sword of Galgano
Piercing eternity.

Galgano, 1148-1181,
a knight-monk of Tuscany

Ouija

She told us not to do it but we did.
The slightest touch of finger and it slid
To letter after letter, then a word
Appeared right there before us, as we heard
My mother sliding toward us in her gown,
And not desirous of her scold or frown,
We pushed the box and board under the beds,
And closed our eyes and covered up our heads,
But giggled all togther as we thought
About the word, a synonym for "caught."

The Dream

One night as I was dreaming
Of lands far, far away,
I saw a green oasis
Just at the close of day.

The sun was falling swiftly
Into the sandy sea,
And nothing had the power
To wreck tranquility.

When suddenly appearing
From north, south, east, and west,
What seemed a sandstorm rising
As on a mighty quest

To drink the living water
Beneath the fronding trees
And nourish on the substance
Provided there by these.

It came, and unrelenting,
It came at rapid pace,
It came in grand precision,
Encircling the space.

But then, as if commanded
By some transcending word,
It slowed its deft advancement.
It stopped, and then I heard

A thunderous order given
And ten by ten they strode
In columns to the fountains—
How silently they rode,

The rich panoply glinting
Bejeweled, like the stars—
A thousand windblown turbans,
A thousand scimitars.

And as that host dismounted
To rest beneath the palm,
I saw majestic splendor—
The army of Islam!

A. E. Housman

With rue his heart was laden,
And I have read his heart,
And he had borne the burden
Of one who lived apart
From all he ever cherished,
And all that he adored,
A lifetime in a tower
Surrounded by the word.

Dead languages and living,
Exacting every phrase,
He ordered out of chaos
The verbally-spent days.
His heart was not in Shropshire,
Though rue can there be found.
Some hearts can take or leave it.
Some carry it around.

A. E. Housman, poet, 1859-1936,
wrote A *Shropshire Lad*

Men, Be Brave

"Men, be brave!" the corporal counseled,
"Combat is not all that bad.
When the whistle blows remember
Dear Old England and be glad."

All along the line they listened,
Then they rose and then they died,
For they met not town or hamlet,
Only guns which had not lied.

If such scenes of native country
Make young soldiers' courage swell,
Then those scenes of every homeland
Decorate the halls of Hell.

If, In Some Places

If, in some places the heart beats faster
Because a child you knew is buried there,
Or here you kissed a lover in the night,
Or learned the awful pain and power of fear:

Do not at all be taken by surprise,
Or misstep once upon this toilsome way,
For hearts so independent of the time
Forever seek such places in their day.

Soon, soon enough the mystery will end,
And you will lie in dark and lonely spaces
To wait for those who stop and pause to hear
Soft whispers in these solitary places.

Peter Quince on the Banjo
(after Wallace Stevens)

My part in that rendition was obscure.
I was accused of doing it for cash.
I never liked my fingers on the keys.
The strings—I am much more at home on these.

Though I confess it was on interplay,
As subtle on the surface as profound.
That talk of ancient evils and intrigues,
A female body walking on the leaves.

The lusty men were hiding in the grass,
And gawked at lovely ladies as they bathed,
Then claimed they saw more than they truly had.
But motives are all pure when left unsaid.

That is another story, long since past.
Now I work on to master things at hand.
Yet I am still a slave to what I see.
I ask Susanna not to cry for me.

Poet Wallace Stevens, 1879-1955,
wrote *Peter Quince at the Clavier*

Veterans Hospital

If I turn to the right
And go a mile or two,
A place for the infirm
Comes suddenly in view.

It is a place for men
Disabled in our wars.
I call them men today,
But once they were mere boys.

Such patriotic youth
Are very, very good
At going where they're told
And doing what they should.

When flags begin to wave,
Aligning armament,
It is not older men
But youth go where they're sent.

And some do not come home,
But some come home to stay
In places down the road
A mile or two away.

I know that I should stop
And spread some joy and cheer
Or anything at all
Might well be welcome there.

But I must travel on,
For I must travel far.
If I turn to the right.
We will not win this war.

I? Awake

I? Awake. I am not sleeping,
Though I tossed an hour or two.
Better to have been in dreamland
Than to dream of what you do.

When you go away all evening,
I admit, I am concerned.
True, it is your pattern lately,
And by now I should have learned.

Gun? It is a gun, my darling.
O, how deep the jealous pine.
See, I place it near your temple.
Sit, my pretty. Rest. Recline.

Sikh Holocaust

I hid my wife and daughter
To keep them from the men
Who raged across our nation
With that demonic grin.

The flower was dipped in nectar,
Where swarmed the bird and bee.
They mocked the failed protector,
Then laughed and set me free.

Your Hands

You say your hands are old, just like your mother's,
That they have seemed that way since you were small.
But let us not compare them to another's,
For I have seen them differently from all.

Before I ever held them in my own,
I know these are the hands that from a book
Of notes and marks and things I had not known
Gave me a Mozart and the strange Bartok.

They taught me Haydn and our dear Chopin,
And Debussy's achievement, "Clair de Lune,"
So delicate and soothing from those hands —
I desecrated whistling as a tune!

I see them now at knitting and at tea,
Our marriage china giving it a flair
Of affluence that we would never see —
But all in fun; we tolerate no air!

I told you once that at my dying bed
Your face would be last thing I would know.
But now I think that what I should have said
Is take my hand and I can safely go.

Vampire

This bleeding from the mouth
Should cause you no alarm.
I am assured by some
It lubricates my charm.

Your lips are red and full.
I give them just a peck.
Now turn your head, sweet lamb.
My first love is the neck.

Encounters

Of all my sad encounters
I think the saddest yet
Was when I took to highway
And saw the sign, Regret.

For when I reached that city,
And there was welcomed in,
I kept what I remembered,
And wished my life again.

Heaven for Spina Bifida

The children do not cry
Because they cannot walk.
They do not roll away
To stop the cutting talk.

The wheelchairs put aside,
The spines are straight and strong.
The children run and jump.
Eternity is long.

www.ingramcontent.com/pod-product-compliance
Lightning Source LLC
LaVergne TN
LVHW051707080426
835511LV00017B/2779